Comparing Minibeasts

# Minibeast Babies

## Charlotte Guillain

Raintre

## www.raintreepublishers.co.uk

Visit our website to find out
more information about
Raintree books.

**To order:**

☎ Phone 0845 6044371
🖨 Fax +44 (0) 865 312263
✉ Email myorders@raintreepublishers.co.uk

Customers from outside the UK please telephone +44 1865 312262

Raintree is an imprint of Capstone Global Library Limited, a company
incorporated in England and Wales having its registered office at 7 Pilgrim
Street, London, EC4V 6LB – Registered company number: 6695582

Edited by Nancy Dickmann and Catherine Veitch
Designed by Joanna Hinton-Malivoire
Picture research by Elizabeth Alexander
Production by Duncan Gilbert and Victoria Fitzgerald
Originated by Heinemann Library
Printed and bound in China by South China Printing
Company Ltd

ISBN 978 0 431 19493 6 (hardback)
14 13 12 11 10
10 9 8 7 6 5 4 3 2 1

ISBN 978 0 431 19500 1 (paperback)
15 14 13 12 11
10 9 8 7 6 5 4 3 2 1

**British Library Cataloguing in Publication Data**
Guillain, Charlotte.
Comparing minibeasts.
Babies.
592.1'39-dc22

**Acknowledgements**
We would would like to thank the following for permission to reproduce
photographs: Alamy p. **13** (© Nigel Cattlin); Ardea.com pp. **6** (© Jim
Frazier-Densey Clyne / Auscape), **9** (© Steve Hopkin), **11** (© Auscape),
**23** (© Auscape); Corbis pp. **7** (© Michael & Patricia Fogden), **17**
(© Clouds Hill Imaging Ltd.); FLPA pp. **8** (© Jeremy Early), **10** (© Mark
Moffett/Minden Pictures), **16** (© Gary K Smith); **22 top** (iStockphoto);
NHPA pp. **4** (N A CALLOW), **14** (A.N.T. PHOTO LIBRARY); Photolibrary
pp. **12** (Mark MacEwen/OSF), **18** (Martin Page/Garden Picture Library),
**15** (JAMES ROBINSON/Animals Animals), **21** (Bryan Reynolds/
Phototake Science), **20** (Juniors Bildarchiv), **23 top** (Mark MacEwen/
OSF), **23 middle bottom** (Martin Page/Garden Picture Library);
Shutterstock pp. **5** (© Cathy Keifer), **19** (© Goran Kapor), **22 left**
(© Matthew Cole), **22 right** (© Vinicius Tupinamba), **23 middle top**
(© Yellowj).

Cover photograph of caterpillars reproduced with permission of
iStockphoto (© Simon Alvinge). Back cover photograph of a Monarch
caterpillar crawling on a milkweed leaf reproduced with permission of
Shutterstock (© Cathy Keifer).

The publishers would like to thank Nancy Harris and Kate Wilson for their
assistance in the preparation of this book.

Every effort has been made to contact copyright holders of material
reproduced in this book. Any omissions will be rectified in subsequent
printings if notice is given to the publishers.

# Contents

# Meet the minibeasts

There are many different types
of minibeasts.

There are many different types of
baby minibeasts.

# Eggs

egg

Some minibeasts lay eggs.

eggs

Butterflies lay eggs on leaves.

eggs

Mosquitoes lay eggs in water.

eggs

Bluebottles lay eggs on food.

silk case

egg

Some spiders put a silk case around
their eggs.

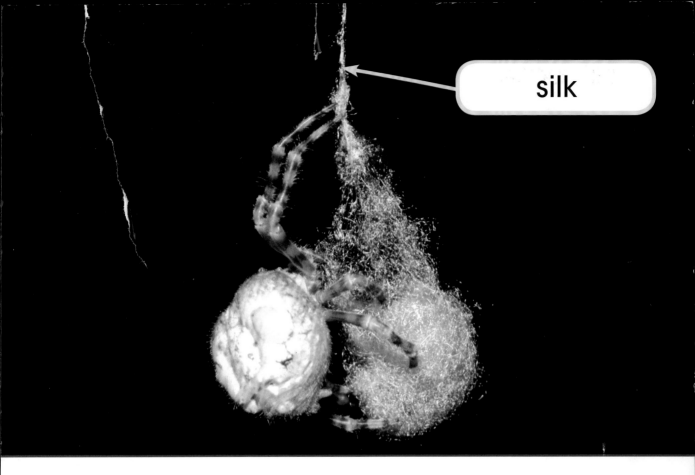

silk

Some spiders hang their eggs from a silk thread.

# Minibeast young

Many young minibeasts hatch
from eggs.

adult woodlouse

young woodlouse

Many young minibeasts look like adult minibeasts.

adult centipede

young centipede

Young centipedes look like
adult centipedes.

young spider

Young spiders look like adult spiders.

# Changing minibeasts

young ladybird

adult ladybird

Some young minibeasts do not look like adult minibeasts.

larvae

Some eggs hatch into larvae.

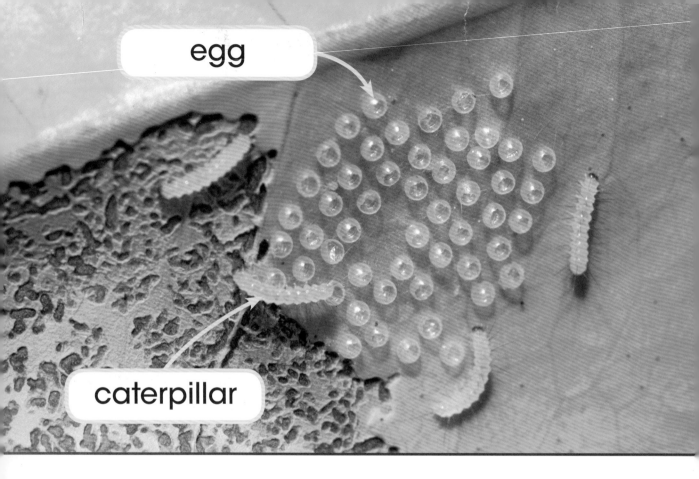

egg

caterpillar

A caterpillar is a type of larva.

A caterpillar grows and changes into a butterfly.

# Caring for minibeast babies

bee larvae

Some insects take care of
their larvae.

young spider

Wolf spiders carry their young on their backs.

# How big?

ladybird

mosquito

spider

Look at how big some of the
minibeasts in this book can be.

# Picture glossary

**hatch**  break out of an egg

**insect**  very small creature with six legs

**larva**  minibeast baby that hatches from an egg. It does not look like an adult. More than one is larvae.

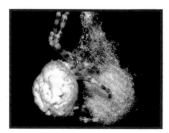
**silk**  soft, strong material made by spiders and other minibeasts

# Index

**Notes to parents and teachers**

**Before reading**

Make a list of minibeasts with the children. Try to include insects, arachnids (e.g. spiders), crustaceans (e.g. woodlice), myriapods (e.g. centipedes and millipedes), earthworms, slugs, and snails. Have they ever seen any minibeast eggs? Do they know what a butterfly egg hatches into?

**After reading**

- Get a butterfly kit for your classroom to watch how caterpillars grow and change into butterflies. Help the children to measure the caterpillars, and examine them under a magnifying glass. Ask the children to make a diary recording how the caterpillars change.
- Between spring and late summer you could go outside and hunt for minibeast eggs. Show the children how to look in soil, under stones, in dead leaves, and on leaves. If they find any eggs ask them to observe and record how many eggs there are, what shape and colour they are, and where exactly they were found.
- If the children find any eggs you could bring them into the classroom and put them into a pot along with some of the soil or leaves on which they were found. Ask the children to watch the eggs every day and see if any minibeasts hatch.